GCSE
English Exam Techniques

a 16-week revision programme

Keith Brindle **John Nield**

Introduction

Your questions answered.

Q: What is the point of this book?
A: The aims of this book are:

- to give a **clear insight** into the skills you need to succeed in GCSE English exams
- to show **when** and **where** those skills need to be demonstrated
- to **practise** those skills, and give the opportunity to **develop** them **on your own**
- to **explain** how your **work is marked** by examiners
- to **provide** a **structured programme** that leads right up to the exams themselves

and, most important of all,

- to **enable you to gain those extra marks** which will improve your chance of **a higher grade.**

Q: But you can't revise English, can you?
A: English may not appear to be a subject with lots of facts, figures or formulae, but, like any other subject, it has component parts and skills that can be practised and learned. This book has a series of structured units which will focus on those parts and skills.

Q: How can this book help me to get a better grade, then?
A: You should work through the book, unit by unit. However, if this is not possible, you can focus on key pages or sections which you – or your teacher – consider to be problematic. As you will see, the book has a clear structure which is easy to follow.

Q: So, how is this revision book structured?
A: There are 16 units (plus a final checklist) – which could fit the 16 weeks before your exam. Each one deals with a key aspect of the English exam, whether it's 'Knowing the Papers' or 'Writing to Argue'. Each Unit is between four to six pages long and is split into four sections:

- the opening section gives **advice** and **information**
- the second section gives **practice**, often in small 'bite-size' tasks
- the third section gives **further practice**, with more developed writing
- the final section provides **extension work** and shows you **how to move up a grade**, using key skills that you, yourself, identify.

Q: Is there anything else to help me?
A: Yes. On many pages, we, the authors of this book (two senior examiners), offer **Examiner's Tips** – that is, key pointers to improve your work. Also, each Unit ends with a **summary** of the main points covered.

Q: Sounds great. When can I get started?
A: That's easy – just turn the page.

Keith Brindle, John Nield

Contents

Unit 1	Knowing the Papers	4
Unit 2	Reading Non-Fiction Texts	8
Unit 3	Reading Media Texts	14
Unit 4	Comparing Non-Fiction and Media Texts	18
Unit 5	Revising Reading Skills	24
Unit 6	Genres	28
Unit 7	A Writing Process for Section B	32
Unit 8	Revising Writing Skills	38
Unit 9	Writing to Argue	42
Unit 10	Writing to Persuade	48
Unit 11	Writing to Advise	54
Unit 12	Writing to Inform	60
Unit 13	Writing to Explain	64
Unit 14	Writing to Describe	68
Unit 15	Revising Poetry from Different Cultures and Traditions	72
Unit 16	Final Revision for English	76
	Your Final Checklist	80

Unit 1 Knowing the Papers

Targets
1. To understand the form of the examination.
2. To know what is tested in English Paper 1.
3. To know what is tested in English Paper 2.

General Information

The AQA/A English course is followed by many candidates, all sitting the same exam as you. It is important, therefore, that you are well prepared: you have a great deal of competition!

English GCSE — details

Coursework: 40% of final mark   20% for written coursework
                                      20% for Speaking and Listening

Examinations: 60% of final mark   30% for Paper 1
                                      30% for Paper 2

Paper 1 lasts for 1 hour 45 minutes
Paper 2 lasts for 1 hour 30 minutes

The English Literature examination, for which you might also be entered, has one paper lasting 1 hour 45 minutes. English Literature is a separate subject and receives a separate grade.

In this book, we will be dealing exclusively with the English examination.

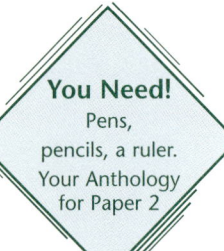

You Need!
Pens, pencils, a ruler.
Your Anthology for Paper 2

What you need for your English examinations

Pens, pencils, a ruler.
Your Anthology for Paper 2.

Dictionaries are not allowed.

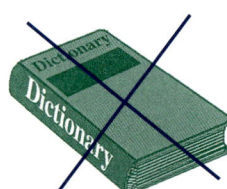

Of course, it is not enough simply to arrive on the day of the examination with the correct equipment.

You will be tested on a range of skills and, to do well, you need to be aware of:
- what is being tested
- what the examiner is looking for
- and how to produce the best answers.

It is vital that you walk into each examination knowing exactly what is expected of you and confident that you can deal with the questions.

English Paper 1

- Lasts for 1 hour 45 minutes.
- Contains two sections, both marked out of 27.
  You should spend about an hour on Section A and 45 minutes on Section B.

FACTS
- Time
- Marks

Section A

Section A requires you to write about two or three texts (non-fiction or media), which will be printed on the paper. There will be one question, broken into three or four different parts. Answer all parts of the question.

Your reading skills are being tested, to see if you can:
- *tell the difference between fact and opinion and evaluate how information is presented*
- *follow an argument, spotting implications and inconsistencies*
- *explain how different texts deal in different ways with the same subject*
- *choose parts of the texts to support your answers*
- *write about how language structure and layout are used*
- *recognise features of media and non-fiction texts.*

FOCUS
Non-Fiction and Media Texts
Testing Reading Skills

If you are presented with two texts, a possible pattern for the questions is:

Question 1 (a)
You will be asked about one of the texts and must select and write about parts of it. This could involve writing about facts or opinions; or explaining certain information; or writing about how an argument is constructed.

Question 1 (b)
This question will look at a different text.
If it is the media text, you might have to write about purpose and audience or presentation and layout.

Question 1 (c)
You will probably have to compare the two texts you have read. You will have to focus on various elements, one of which might be the language used.
You might be asked which text is more successful in what it sets out to do.

Minutes = Marks
EXAMINER'S TIP!

There are 27 marks in Section A: see how many marks are available for each part of the question and spend **2 minutes for each mark**. If five marks are available, spend 10 minutes on that part of the question.

Section B

Section B requires you to write about a subject that has some connection with the texts used in Section A. You choose one question to answer. You will have to:
- **argue** (Question 2)
- **persuade** (Question 3)
- **advise** (Question 4)

or
- **blend the skills together** (Question 5).

Your writing skills are being tested and you will be marked on your:
- *content: the ideas and information you include*
- *ability to write for a given audience and purpose*
- *ability to organise writing, so that what you say flows effectively and logically*
- *paragraphing*
- *language*
- *accuracy: sentences, spelling and expression.*

You are advised to write about **two sides**. Spend:
- 5 minutes planning
- 35 minutes writing
- 5 minutes checking.

English Paper 2

- Lasts for 1 hour 30 minutes.
- Contains two sections, both marked out of 27.
  You should spend about 45 minutes on each section.

Section A

The questions are related to the **Anthology**. Bring it with you to the examination. Your school is unlikely to have spare copies.

For 2004, your Anthology can contain brief annotations, but you must not write sentences in it. After 2004, no annotations are allowed!

Your reading skills are being tested, and in your answers you will be expected to:
- *respond to the poems*
- *explain what they are saying*
- *use appropriate parts of the poems to explain your points*
- *compare and contrast poems*
- *write about the language, how poems are presented on the page and how they are constructed*
- *comment on the way language is used differently in the poems.*

You will be asked about what the poems have to say and how they say it.

The poems are drawn from different cultures and traditions.
You will be offered a choice of one from two questions. You will have to write about two or three poems.

Section B

This section tests the same writing skills as Section B in Paper 1.
Choose **one** question and write about **two** sides. You must write to:

- **inform** (Question 3)
- **explain** (Question 4)
- **describe** (Question 5)

or

- **blend the skills together** (Question 6).

Spend:
- **5** minutes planning
- **35** minutes writing
- **5** minutes checking.

Planning

Writing

Checking

FOCUS
Inform
Explain
Describe

Re-read this Unit, then working in pairs test each other:

Knowing the Papers

How much have you remembered?

1. Which examination paper involves the Anthology?
2. How many poems from Different Cultures and Traditions will you have to write about?
3. What kinds of essays will be expected from you in English Paper 1?
4. In English Paper 1, Section A, how many texts are you likely to have to read?
5. If, in Paper 1, Section A, a question carries 10 marks, how long should you spend answering it?
6. How long do you have to answer each paper?
7. What are you allowed to write inside your Anthology?
8. How should you divide up the time available to write essays in Section B?
9. When comparing texts in Paper 1, Section A, what aspects of the texts are you likely to be asked about?
10. How many marks are available for each section of both papers?

Unit 2 Reading Non-Fiction Texts

To learn about Paper 1, Section A:
1. To learn what is tested.
2. To learn how to respond to the questions.

Section A of Paper 1 requires you to examine two or three non-fiction or media texts: these could be newspaper articles; magazine articles or leaflets; biographies or autobiographies; web pages; letters; advertisements; diary entries or obituaries.

To prepare for this examination, you must read widely and regularly.

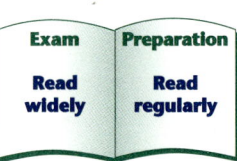

There will probably be at least one part of the question on a non-fiction text; another on a media text; and one that requires you to compare texts. This unit deals with non-fiction texts; media texts are dealt with in Unit 3, and comparisons in Unit 4.

What will you be asked about?

The style of questions varies slightly from year to year; however, at some point you will be expected to write about:
- **facts** in the texts – things that are certain, that can be proved, that have happened or that exist beyond any doubt
- **opinions** in the texts – people's views or beliefs, their interpretation of events, how they see things, what someone considers to be the truth
- and **how facts and opinions are used**.

You will also have to:
- **select appropriate material** – find proof for your ideas, quoting if necessary
- **follow an argument** – know what is said and how
- **analyse the language used**
- **write about presentation and layout**: how the material is set out on the page. (Language, presentation and layout will be dealt with in Units 3 and 4.)

Always read questions carefully and underline or highlight the important words, so you concentrate on what is required:

e.g. <u>Explain</u> in your <u>own words</u> the writer's <u>opinion</u> of football.

Read this newspaper report.

PRACTICE

Offenders reformed by victims

New method proves effective in changing criminals' lives

The Home Office recently released details of an experiment which has brought together young offenders and their victims. The face-to-face meetings have been producing remarkable results.

Statistics show that most young offenders reoffend within two years. Incredibly, the figure can be as high as 89% for 15 and 16 year olds. This is a situation which has been allowed to continue for years because there has been no system in place, to change the ways of the criminals. Imprisonment punishes them, but does not make them reform their ways.

However, the Leeds Probation Service has been trialling a new approach. Victim and offender sit down together, and the victim learns why the offender committed the crime.

More importantly, the offender has to take responsibility for what he has done. Put simply: the offenders, when they have to listen to the sufferings of the victims, realise the errors of their ways. They get to know the real person they have hurt. PC Dove, a peacemaking mediator, says: "You can turn someone's life around. Often, these are not bad young people; they simply did a bad thing."

PC Dove and those working with him seem to have a point: 68% of youngsters involved in the project had not reoffended after two years. One boy summed up what had happened to him: "My life's changed 'cos I made it change." And that seems to sum up the success of the venture.

Task 1

How are facts used to prove that the scheme has been successful?
Write down *three facts* and explain their effect.

(3 marks)

The important words are <u>facts (3)</u>, <u>prove</u>, <u>successful</u> and <u>explain their effect</u>.
Here the writer uses statistics to prove his point.

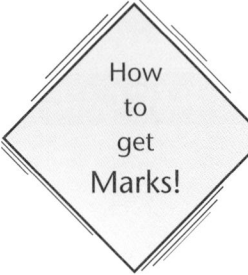

How to get Marks!

Consider the mark scheme:
- 'Statistics show that most young offenders reoffend within two years'
  – implies old system does not work
- 'the figures can be as high as 89% for 15 and 16 year olds'
  – high figure suggests change is vital
- '68% of youngsters involved in the project had not reoffended after 2 years'
  – new system clearly seems better.

Task 2

If you missed any of these points, check back and see where they came from.

Ensure that if you were asked a question like this, you would know how to answer it.

Task 3

An F Tier question:

Find four opinions and show how the writer uses them. (4 marks)

You might begin:
1. 'The face-to-face meetings have been producing remarkable results.'
   Here, the writer uses 'remarkable' to convince us that the new system is working.
2. ... .

Complete the answer.

Task 4

A harder question which could be for the F Tier, but is more likely to appear on the H Tier paper:

How does the writer use opinions? (4 marks)

In this case, find the opinions about **what was wrong with the old system** and those which say **the new one is better** – and show **how** the writer uses the opinions to **convince the reader**.

For example:
'... Later, the writer says: "the offenders ... realise the errors of their ways".
This implies that the system always works and that all offenders are changed by the experience. It is stated like a fact, and might well convince the reader ...'

4 marks = 8 minutes
EXAMINER'S TIP!

Always notice how many marks are available, and spend 2 minutes for each mark. That will give you time to answer all the questions!

If there was a question about **following the argument** in the article, you might write about:
- what is said
- how facts and opinions are used effectively
- how discourse markers move the argument along ('However', 'More importantly', 'Often')
- what is quoted
- how the opening and concluding paragraphs convince the reader ('Both the opening and concluding paragraphs sound convincing and make the scheme seem successful …').

Key Features

With another text, you might want to write about:
- humour
- anecdote (short stories used to illustrate a point)
- examples (evidence for what is said)
- rhetorical questions (which are used for effect and do not require an answer – e.g. 'Who cares?')
- emotive language (which touches our emotions – e.g. 'poor, starving children')
- similes and metaphors
- variety of sentence length and so on.

Task 5

Choose any newspaper or magazine article of a similar length to the one on page 9.

Use the ideas above as a checklist, and identify how the argument has been constructed.

Extension work: shaping

To gain better grades, it is not enough just to find the correct information – you are expected to 'use' the details, to write convincing answers. Examiners call this 'shaping' the material.

Shaping for Grading
EXAMINER'S TIP!

'**Shaping**' means:
- explaining what you have found
- rearranging the material for the examiner
- writing about information, rather than just listing it.

Shaping

Read this newspaper report:

Fake Lords Mock our Visitors

To get our own back on the Americans might appear praiseworthy – but is it? For years now they have looked down on their 'cute little old cousins' in Europe so it can be a delight to see a Texan looking foolish. Especially if he wears a large Stetson hat and checked trousers, of course.

However, a scam to trick Americans and take their cash under false pretences has been discovered, and are the police laughing? Not at all.

J.C. Tucker, a Texan oil baron, has complained of being defrauded of over £2000 by Lord Wacket of Windelbury. He paid the cash to stay on his Lordship's country estate for a week, as one of 20 house guests. But he realised, during a £400-a-head banquet, that his host was not in fact Lord Wacket, but an actor, Timothy Dalford. He was playing the part of Wacket for the holiday season.

The police sent in a top team. Their enquiries have produced

Timothy Dalford

four arrests, and an extended investigation. A probe of other mansions in surrounding counties has found that over 40% run scams along similar lines. Americans are the main targets. "They can afford it, though," said an admirer of Lord Wacket.

J.C. Tucker is in Cannes, recovering, and does not wish to comment.

The writer here does not seem worried by the fraudulent activities.
Question: How does he try to persuade us to treat the incident lightly?

An answer should refer to those features mentioned at the top of page 11.

Here are three extracts from candidates:

> **F Grade**
> The writer tells us about how Americans are good to laugh at. One paid a lot of money to Lord Wacket and he was cheated. 40% run scams along similar lines. The police have arrested some people and J.C. Tucker has gone to Cannes to recover …
>
> **C Grade**
> The writer mocks the Americans who wear Stetson hats and checked trousers and deserve to be cheated out of their money. J.C. Tucker is rich because he goes to Cannes, so we do not feel sorry for him. In fact, someone is quoted as saying Americans can afford it, so, again, we have no sympathy. There are also facts to make us laugh …
>
> **A Grade**
> The article opens with a rhetorical question, challenging us to think about our attitude to the Americans. Then without mentioning the fraudulent activity, we are offered the opinion that Americans patronise us ('cute little cousins'), but that they themselves are figures of fun, judging by the clothes they wear. Similarly, when we later hear the facts about how much they were paying to be Wacket's guests, they seem to deserve no sympathy at all …

Task 6

Comparing Grades

1. Look at the 'F Grade' response. Is the candidate explaining the writer's technique? How has the candidate used the information in the passage?

2. Why is the 'C Grade' response better?

3. Say why the final extract is the best. Examine how:
   - the candidate selects features of the article
   - the candidate responds to the material, rather than just repeating what it says (e.g. 'challenging us to think')
   - the material is shaped.

Task 7

Continue the 'A Grade' response, using the skills you have just identified.

Examiner's Summary

- Read widely, to develop your understanding and skills, and practise on other texts.

- Prepare to write about how facts and opinions are used and how arguments are put together.

- Always answer the question that has been set and notice how many marks are available.

- On the H Tier, aim to shape your writing.

Unit 3   Reading Media Texts

Targets   To focus on:
1. Purpose and audience.
2. How layout and presentation are used.
3. The effect of language in media texts.

Many non-fiction texts come from the world of the media: articles, reports, advertisements, and so on. It is quite possible that all the texts you meet on Paper 1, Section A will be media texts.

FOCUS Emphasis

However, when examining a piece of writing **as** media text, the emphasis is likely to be upon:
- purpose – why the text was produced
- audience – the people for whom it is written
- how layout and presentation are used
- the effectiveness of the language
- how well the text fulfils its purpose
- how appropriately it appeals to its target audience.

Consider this example:

Task 1

Decide:
- what exactly is the purpose and target audience for this product
- how it is attempting to appeal to its audience
- how successful it is likely to be. Give reasons.

Response 1:
'The advert is for a chocolate bar you wouldn't give your granny. They are trying to get you to buy it. It is called "Blitzed" and on the advert there is a picture of a boy who looks weird. People like that will probably buy it ...'

Response 2:
'Any advertisement tries to get you to buy a product, and this one is no different. The chocolate bar is new and is clearly being aimed at young people. The picture is to make you think people who buy the bar are different from the older generation – free to be what they want to be; and even the name of the bar will attract the target audience, because "Blitzed" sounds like some kind of new drug ...'

Task 2

1. Which response is better? Why?
2. What else might have been added to Response 2?
3. How good is your response, in comparison?

Television standards topple
'No nourishment for couch potatoes,' says report.

The latest review of television standards makes depressing reading. According to Telview, the independent viewing commission, we are being subjected to more repeats and more 'dumbing down' of programmes than ever before. Rather than liberating our televiewing habits, digital TV is giving us only programmes we have seen before and a diet of cartoons and cheap-to-make 'rubbish': our minds are not stimulated but we still do not turn off ...

Task 3

1. What is the purpose and audience for this text?
2. How is language used by the writer?

Purpose
To entertain? To inform?
To persuade? To mock?

Audience
Children? Parents? Teachers?

Unit 3 Reading Media Texts

Use Technical Language
EXAMINER'S TIP!

To write about how the text is set out on the page – layout and presentation – and language, you need the sort of vocabulary listed in Unit 5 and Unit 6.

When analysing layout and presentation, always try to:
- Bear in mind the target audience.
- Examine the particular effect of a picture:
  - Does it make us sympathetic/angry/suspicious/laugh? Why/how?
  - Would a different picture create a different impact?
- Decide why particular colours have been used:
  - red might indicate anger, or violence or love or danger or …
  - blue might seem very conservative or restful or …
  - green might seem peaceful or environmentally friendly or …
- Judge the possible effects of text boxes, headings, sub-headings, particular fonts and their size and so on.

FOCUS Layout Presentation

When analysing the language used, always try to:
- Bear in mind the target audience.
- Say why particular words or phrases have been used, rather than just listing devices.
- Use the sort of techniques you are familiar with from your study of literature: select linguistic features, and say exactly what effect on the reader each one has, or is intended to have (For example: 'The writer puts "dumbing down" and "rubbish" in inverted commas. They are selective and critical quotations which draw the reader's attention and emphasise the report's attitude to modern television.')

FOCUS Language

Extension Work

Read this review of a new release by Foxfur:

The Fur's still flying:
'Cockatrice' released this week.

Incredibly, after over 20 years as an 'underground' band, Foxfur are still being courted by the top record labels. And, on this latest showing from the hottest rock property never to have a hit single, they look set to continue for many years more.

Unit 3 *Reading Media Texts*

For their latest CD, 'Cockatrice', they have produced 12 tracks which move from the sultry R & B strains of Van Morrison in his prime to echoes of Ozzy Osbourne and then to the control of Toploader. Yet it never turns into some kind of sad and varied sampler: the lead vocals of Jimmy Forest never weaken, and the distinctive harmonies of Jenny and Sue Lin tie the tracks together.

It is hard to imagine any of the new bands around lasting so long or, indeed, producing such high-quality music over such a long period. Foxfur are setting off on yet another world tour, to promote 'Cockatrice'. Get the album and catch the tour: they're better than ever and you won't be disappointed.

Task 4

How effective is this review?

Consider:
- its purpose and target audience
- how layout and presentation and language have been used.

> In this answer, 'evaluate' the material: *judge* whether it is good – and decide whether it could be improved.

Task 5

1. Write and present a review of a CD by D. J. Spin for a teenage audience.
2. Bearing in mind the purpose and audience, explain your choice of:
   - layout and presentation
   - language.

Examiner's Summary

- When examining media texts, always concentrate on the purpose and audience.
- Prepare to write about layout and presentation and language.
- Do not simply list features: try to analyse how they have been used and the effect they have on the reader.

Unit 4 Comparing Non-Fiction and Media Texts

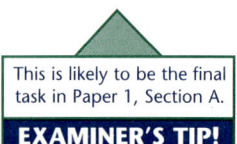

To learn how to:
1. Read the question carefully.
2. Make brief notes for each bullet point, referring to both texts.
3. Find proof for your points and employ technical terms.
4. Write effectively, explaining the material and its effects.

> **EXAMINER'S TIP!**
> This is likely to be the final task in Paper 1, Section A.

See Unit 1 page 5 for more information.

Read carefully	means	check the main requirement of the question, then what the bullet points require.
Make brief notes	means	write a quick plan, using the bullet points as sub-headings.
Find proof for your points	means	include in your plan short quotations from the texts as evidence, and use technical terms you have learnt.
Develop your points	means	explain details, don't just list them.

Stage 1: Read the question carefully

The bullet points lead you through a comparison of the texts. You might be asked

- to write about **purpose** and **audience**, **content**, **language**, **facts** and **opinions**, **layout** and **presentation**, and the **success** of the texts

or

- to **focus** on just **some of these elements**.

Stage 2: Make brief notes

- Organise notes using the bullets as sub-headings.
- Cover all bullet points and both texts.
- Make your notes precise and detailed.

> *In the exam, there will be little time to plan.*
>
> *However, when practising, this technique will develop your skills.*

Stage 3: Find proof and use technical terms

Do not copy out long quotations. Highlight or underline the quotations you need on the texts and make a brief reference to them in your plan.

Choose some technical terms which fit the texts you are looking at. For example: *factual, opinion, subjective, objective, rhetorical, emotive, irony, metaphor, simile, alliteration, headline, italics,* etc. See Unit 5 (page 26) for a more detailed list.

FOCUS: Comparing Texts

Stage 4: Write your answer, developing your points

- Do not simply copy out your plan. Discuss points of layout or language, saying why the writer has used them and whether they are effective.
- Do not forget that you are comparing the two texts and judging them against each other.

Read the newspaper report below.

PRACTICE

Students bored to breaking point

"I just said what everyone else was thinking," says student excluded for speaking out.

Is it time our outdated approaches to schooling came into line with the modern world? That is the question being debated in a small town in the Midlands after a fifteen-year-old pupil was excluded from school for saying he found assembly boring.

Elliott: "I'm no troublemaker."

Elliott Byron had never been in serious trouble throughout his life at Durnhill High School in Barton, Warwickshire, until he dared to write to the local paper, complaining about his headteacher's assemblies. Then he was suspended.

"I come to school to learn, not to be bored every morning," said Elliott. And, despite the fact that most children feel the same way about assembly, Mrs Garland, his headteacher, was not amused.

Elliott is unrepentant: "I'm only saying what the others say. But the teachers are treating me like a bully or a vandal. I thought we had the right to speak out in this country. The other children say I'm a hero now, so I'm not going to say sorry. Why should I?"

Now read this autobiographical extract:

From 'My Way' by David Sampson

I eventually gave up teaching because I found that, increasingly, the pupils were becoming like their parents. They challenged everything I said and believed they had the right to do as they wished. I have always believed that a child is in school to be taught and to be made into a future citizen of a country of which we should all be proud. Yet, if the adults behave with no consideration for others and their children learn that way of thinking from them, what hope is there for the poor teachers?

Schools need to be given more power over their pupils. They need to be supported by the government. They need to be supported by the police. They need to concentrate on improving the nation's morals. Daily acts of worship need to be compulsory and must take place. There should be more emphasis on Religious Education. We have turned into a society with no faith in God and no interest in others. Unless we act quickly to turn the tide, we could find that there is no way back to decency and the belief that the world can be a better place.

Task 1

Make notes on the following question:

Compare the two extracts. In your answer, discuss:

- the layout of each extract
- the use made of facts and opinions
- how the language tries to capture our interest
- what the writers think about schools, assemblies and the rights of children
- which extract persuades us most successfully.

Your notes on 'Students bored to breaking point' should
look something like this:

Layout	• headline • sub-heading • columns • photograph • short, journalistic, paragraphs
Facts	• excluded for saying assembly boring • letter to paper criticised head's assemblies
Opinions	• kind of child Elliott is said to be • what the writer chooses to quote from Elliott • writer's phrasing: 'dared', 'most children feel the same', 'Garland not amused', etc.
Language	• newspaper style (sentences begin with 'And' and 'But') • alliteration in the heading ('bored to breaking point') • use of quotation: generally subjective report • simile ('like a bully or a vandal') • metaphor ('I'm a hero') • rhetorical questions ('Why should I?')
What the writer thinks	• suggests approaches 'outdated' • Elliott brave to oppose assemblies ('dared') • only Elliott quoted ('I'm no troublemaker') • says others agree with Elliott: opinion given without proof • picture chosen to make Elliott seem respectable
Success	• easy to follow • sense that one student is bravely standing against the school system • fight is being waged by someone who 'is not a troublemaker'

Task 2

Develop your first set of notes on the article 'My Way', so that they are as detailed as the ones above.

You can examine non-fiction and media texts by using the headings above whenever you read. The more you practise, the quicker you will be able to do it!

> To achieve 'C' standard or above, you must clearly compare the texts, using words like: 'on the other hand', 'however', 'Just as Text 1 ..., so Text 2 ...', 'whereas', and so on.

Task 3

Now write a full answer to the original question in essay style, comparing the two texts and using the two sets of notes.

Extension Work: Assessing your response

Task 4

Apply this mark scheme to your work and decide which grade description most closely matches your work.

F Grade

You

- concentrated on just one text
- mentioned layout/presentation, by saying that there is a picture, or columns or headings
- said the writers use facts and opinions to convince us (you might have selected one or two)
- said something about the language, perhaps that it is hard to understand, or easy
- said what the extracts are about
- said which one you liked best.

C Grade

You

- compared the texts, using words like: 'similarly', 'whereas', 'however', 'in contrast'.
- mentioned various aspects of layout/presentation, saying how they affect the reader (e.g. 'This draws our attention to ...')
- picked out facts and opinions, saying what the writer intended (e.g. 'Elliott is made to seem ...')
- quoted words or phrases, saying how they affect the reader (e.g. 'This makes us think that ...')
- showed the differences in the writers' opinions
- assessed their success, bearing in mind the things you had already discussed in the answer.

A Grade

You

- were able to consider and compare both texts throughout
- discussed layout/presentation and language, tying your comments to the writers' intentions (e.g. 'Because the writer wants everyone to feel sorry for Elliott, he ...'; 'In contrast, the second writer is appealing to a more intellectual audience, so he ...')
- commented precisely and in detail on layout/presentation and language (e.g. 'These short sentences use a repetitive structure to build to a climax ...')
- discussed the balance between fact and opinion and how the reader is persuaded by the mixture
- assessed the writers' views, blending your comments into an assessment of how successful each was, but using your own phrases and sentence structures (e.g. 'David Sampson's subjective analysis of the situation convinces the reader because he allows no room for argument. The paragraphs themselves seem solid like building blocks ...').

Task 5

If your answer did not merit an A Grade, try again, using the mark scheme to guide your efforts.

Examiner's Summary

- This question carries many marks.
- Spend 2 minutes for each mark awarded.
- Respond to each bullet point.
- Answer in detail, and explain effects; don't just repeat the information contained in the texts.
- Prepare for the question by examining non-fiction and media texts before the examination, looking for features highlighted in this unit.

Good comparison = good grade

Unit 5 Revising Reading Skills

In order to read effectively and follow an argument you will need to:
1. Locate facts and recognise opinions.
2. Answer questions precisely.
3. Quote appropriately.
4. Explain clearly.
5. Use a technical vocabulary.
6. Write at an appropriate length.

Skill 1: Locating facts and recognising opinions

A fact is a fixed piece of information, that is beyond dispute, and can be proved; an opinion is a belief that cannot be completely measured or proved.

Examples:

Fact: English is a subject taught in schools

Opinion: All English teachers are beautiful

FOCUS
Facts
Opinions
Precision

Task 1

Read the following extract then write down five facts and five opinions:

London is the capital of Great Britain. It lures tourists from around the world because it is famous for its historical past, its buildings and the welcome it gives: it has Buckingham Palace, the Houses of Parliament, Big Ben and Trafalgar Square. More recently, it has become well known for hosting the largest marathon in Great Britain and for the London Eye. Three words sum up the London experience: history, heritage and hospitality.

Skill 2: Answering questions precisely

You are expected to read questions accurately and to give the information that is asked for. As in the example below, underline or highlight keywords on the question paper.

What <u>impression</u> of London is the writer trying to create? How are <u>facts</u> and <u>opinions</u> used to create the impression?

Task 2

Now write about:
- what sort of facts are chosen and why (does the writer write about night life? shopping?)
- what sort of phrasing is used to put across the writer's opinion and the effect he or she is seeking.

Remember!

| • Don't simply list facts and opinions. | • Write about the mood the writer wants the reader to experience. | • Show how the writer blends facts and opinions to promote that feeling. |

Skill 3: Quoting appropriately

Quotations should be brief, appropriate and necessary.
They should be placed in quotation marks.
If longer than three words, they should be written on a new line.
They usually come after a point you make, as a way of proving it.
They can be followed by more detailed explanation.

Quotations
Alliteration

Task 3

How does the writer use alliteration at the end of the passage?

Explain the effect of the words 'history, heritage and hospitality', then quote the phrase. Start with 'The writer uses alliteration in the final sentence in order to ...'

Skill 4: Explaining clearly

This will save time, avoid confusion and collect marks.

Read the following confusing sentences:

'He says that when something is thrown across the class even if it is a girl, a boy gets the blame.'
'They went driving for a while and hoped to bump into their friend.'
'When the disease broke out, they closed the school because they had to catch it early.'

Explaining clearly will:
- save time
- avoid confusion
- collect marks

Task 4

Write down what the writers intended to say, and what each sentence actually suggests.

Skill 5: Using a technical vocabulary

You could not talk about a tennis match without using words like 'net', 'serve', 'set' and so on. In the same way, you need the correct words to comment precisely on texts.

Look at these words. Do you know what each means?

Style/language:
Standard English, conversational, formal, argumentative, persuasive, factual, opinionated, informative, patronising, journalistic, subjective, objective, facts, figures, metaphors, similes, alliteration, onomatopoeia, emotive, rhetorical, repetition, quotation, irony.

Presentation/layout:
bullet points, columns, headings, sub-headings, illustrations, diagrams, italics, bold print, font, justified, centred, logos, icons, symbols, headlines, margin, byline, indent, photographs, prose, verse, image, foreground, background, shot, frame, angle, connotation.

Use: a dictionary or ask a teacher

Task 5

a) Select three words you do not understand and find out what they mean.
b) Write three sentences, using one of the words in each, to show you can use them effectively.

E.g. *The way the politician dealt with the teenage protester was very patronising, when she said he had done his best but should leave politics to 'grown-ups'.*

Terms Mean Top Grades
EXAMINER'S TIP!

Revise technical terms, such as the ones in the list above, the night before English Paper 1. Used correctly, they will impress the examiner.

Skill 6: Writing at an appropriate length

- Always check how many marks are available for a question or part-question.

- This information is clearly presented at the right-hand side of the paper, beside the question.

- As a general rule, you should spend twice as many minutes on each question as there are marks for it. There are 27 marks available for Paper 1, Section A. As you have an hour to complete the answers, spend 6 minutes reading the paper and checking your work: that leaves 54 minutes for 27 marks.

Extension Work: Writing about the success of texts

Having examined two or more texts in Section A of Paper 1, you might be asked:
- which is the most successful

or
- which writer puts across a message most effectively.

The best answers discuss the purpose of a text and judge the effectiveness of its:
- language
- presentation and layout.

FOCUS: Successful Texts

The answer becomes a blend of the skills we have been practising.

Read these three conclusions to a comparison question based on two articles about old people. Each conclusion is by a different student.

> **Extract 1 (Grade F):**
> *I thought the writer was boring all the way through the article. She didn't tell me anything I wanted to know and I don't think anyone else would be interested unless they were very old. I like to read things that are full of life and about what young people are thinking.*
>
> **Extract 2 (Grade C):**
> *The writer used language really effectively and made you think about the subject. The way she used headings drew your attention to the different parts of her argument. She had set out to inform the reader about the problems facing old people and did it very well. I am sure that her approach will have won over many young people, because she did not talk down at them.*
>
> **Extract 3 (Grade A):**
> *Since the writer was attempting to convince young people that the old need our help, she made her article suitably appealing. The three columns represented the three strands of her argument; she varied her style, to capture the way youngsters talk; and she brought to life the dilemmas for old people without ever sounding patronising. Young people can empathise with the old if they are not made to feel guilty. This writer clearly understood how to influence her readers.*

Task 6

a) Why would Extract 2 be awarded a higher grade than Extract 1?
b) List the qualities of Extract 3 that you cannot find in the other two.

Examiner's Summary

- Regularly read a range of non-fiction and media texts before the exam.
- Read the question carefully and do what it asks.
- Unless you are asked to list information, try to analyse text, rather than just repeating what it says.
- Always check how many marks are available for each question and spend the right amount of time on it.

Unit 6 Genres

Targets To focus on how writing is made appropriate for different purposes and audiences through the use of:
1. layout
2. style and language.

Paper 1, Section A
For this section you must:
- **recognise** genres
- **show how layout** and **language** are **used**.

Paper 1, Section B
For this section you must:
- **produce** writing in **specified genres**.

During lessons, you will have come across many different genres – that is, types of text. The following two key elements are vital in recognising and writing in different genres.

Element 1 — Layout

Make sure you consider the different elements of presentation, such as:
- columns
- headlines
- sub-headings
- photographs
- illustrations
- boxes
- different paragraph lengths
- italics
- bold type
- various fonts
- letter format

and so on.

You must know **how** and **when** to use these devices.

Element 2 — Style/Language

Depending on topic, purpose and audience, be aware that style can vary. It can be:
- formal or informal
- instructive
- personal
- factual
- reflective
- informative
- persuasive
- technical

and so on.

You must **recognise** different styles and be able to **reproduce** them.

Together, these two elements make the genre. For example, personal writing, presented in chronological day-by-day sequence, in continuous prose = diary.

Layout

Task 1

Read the three blocks of text below.

Riding bikes can be dangerous:
- traffic does not leave enough space
- child cyclists, in particular, have little road sense
- children often show off
- brakes can be faulty
- many do not have lights or wear helmets
- road safety teaching is often poor
- there are too few cycle lanes.

Statistics are frightening:
- nine out of ten young cyclists know virtually nothing of *The Highway Code*
- over 60% of parents are happy to let children cycle without helmets
- 50% of motorists say they narrowly avoided a cyclist in the last month
- 89% of cyclists say they have nearly been knocked off in the last month.

Remedies needed:
- cycle paths
- better government transport policy
- driver and cyclist education
- consideration by road users
- speed reductions for cars.

Task 2

Plan two texts – one for each of the following:

- a leaflet for primary school children about road safety
- a magazine article aimed at parents on the same subject.

Sketch your layouts, considering the use of columns, boxes, etc.
Write **headings** in full; otherwise, show briefly **what you would include**, where, and the language you would use.

Layout & Style/Language = Genre
REMEMBER!

Task 3

For each layout, write *four* reasons why you included particular features.
Look at these examples for the primary leaflet.

Primary Leaflet

1. I used the cartoon because …
2. The short paragraphs were supposed to …

PRACTICE

Language styles

As you know, words and expressions must:
- be chosen with care
- suit the purpose and audience.

Read this news item:

> Yesterday, in Plymouth, Steven Varley, a 19-year-old electrician, won what was probably the strangest competition ever organised in Great Britain. He managed to swallow 75 pickled gherkins in less than 5 minutes, despite hanging upside down from a 60ft-high crane. He beat five other competitors, who only managed to eat 60 gherkins between them. A delighted Steven said he had been training for two months. However, he advised young children not to try to copy him. He does not wish to be responsible for young people falling out of bedroom windows.

Task 4

Headline writing

Write headlines for this story, one each for:

1. A tabloid newspaper
2. A broadsheet newspaper
3. A teenage magazine
4. *Pickles Express*: the trade magazine for grocery departments

Task 5

Read the following extracts. In each case:

a) Write down what genre you think each comes from.
b) List the words or phrases used which are typical of the particular genre.

1. Jones won the ball and, on the stroke of half time, volleyed it into the top corner. The stadium erupted.
2. My darling, each moment without you seems an hour.
3. Quite simply, politicians must act. As we hear regularly in parliament, the Third World is crippled with debt; but when are Western democracies going to show common sense and compassion?
4. Do not think this is a problem you cannot overcome. You can be certain that he is suffering too. Together, you can come through it and your relationship will be stronger.
5. Our product is brighter, cleaner and tougher. It is the future.
6. A man was arrested yesterday for the theft of 200 boxes of designer trainers in Derby last April.

Task 6

For each of the extracts, write the next sentence, continuing in the same style.

Unit 6 Genres

Extension Work: Letter writing

There is often a question in Section B that involves letter writing.

Task 7

Redraft the following letter. There is no need to change the main ideas, but make it appropriate by changing the:
- layout
- style.

Set it out as a **formal letter**, with an argument to persuade the Prime Minister.

> 17 Railway Cuttings,
> Stanwell,
> Chiselholme
> CH9 8RN
>
> 7 March
>
> Dear Tony,
>
> You look like a nice man and I am having trouble with the headteacher at my local school, so I'm writing to you for help. As my friend Eric said, "If the Prime Minister can't help you, what's the use of voting?" Eric's just been voted on to the local fishing club's fund-raising committee, and I trust him. Anyway, that's why I'm writing to you.
>
> You see, the headteacher has just brought in a new rule about the colour of students' hair, and my daughter has had her hair dyed blue and he won't let her go back to lessons until she changes it and she says she won't. I don't think her education should be stopped just because she has got blue hair, do you?
>
> Can you have a word with him? His name's Moorby. He won't listen to me. You believe in fairness, and I think you might be able to do the trick.
>
> Let me know what you think.
>
> Cheers,
>
> Stella Brittan (Mrs)

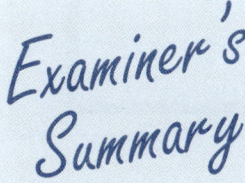

- Read widely, to develop knowledge of different genres.
- Analyse text, by considering intended purpose and audience.
- When writing, make layout and language appropriate for the question.

Unit 7 A Writing Process for Section B

1. To identify purpose and audience.
2. To plan by
   • structuring a response
   • using a 'language palette' to enrich your writing.
3. To write accurately.
4. To check properly.

FACTS
• Time
• Length

Section B of both Paper 1 and Paper 2 involves writing continuously, at some length. In each examination, you are allowed **45 minutes** to plan and produce a response of about **two sides** in length.

Those who write *much more* are likely to be less controlled and to make more errors. Those who write *much less* are unlikely to include enough detail to merit higher grades.

These responses produce half your examination marks in English – 30% of your final total – so it is essential that you have **a Writing Process**: a clear system which:
● you can use every time and gives you confidence
● gives your writing a structure
● allows you to develop your ideas fluently.

Skill 1: Identification of purpose and audience

It is essential that you identify the purpose and audience.

The purpose	The audience
This is the reason for writing; it is the *item* you have been asked to produce: a *letter about homelessness*, an *article about the dangers of fireworks*, etc.	This is the person/people for whom you are writing: *teenagers, old people*, etc.

Skill 2: Planning

You are advised to spend 5 minutes planning your response. Your plan must be detailed and organised, involving key ideas and essential vocabulary.

Invest 5 minutes every time: the better the plan, the better the writing.

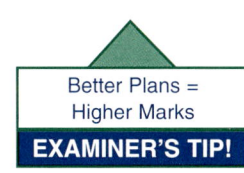

Skill 3: Writing

Follow your plan, otherwise time has been wasted and organisation will be poor.

Skill 4: Checking

You should spend 5 minutes checking your work for errors and adding anything you have missed. Read your response in your head, but as if you were reading it out loud: it will be easier to spot poor expression, missing words and punctuation and incorrect spellings.

How to follow the process

Skill 1: Identification of purpose and audience

Underline or highlight the purpose and audience in the question. This will help you to stay 'on track' as you plan and write.

Read the following exam questions:

> **Question 1:**
> Write an article for an old people's magazine, persuading the readers to take care in the kitchen.
>
> **Question 2:**
> Write a set of instructions for primary school children, telling them about necessary safety rules for the home.

Question 1:

The audience

Write an article for an old people's magazine, persuading the reader to take care in the kitchen.

The purpose and item

Unit 7 A *Writing* Process for Section B   33

Task 1

Write down the purpose, item and audience for Question 2.

You will see immediately why careful planning is necessary.

With more areas of the home to deal with in Question 2, examination time would have to be used differently. Kitchen safety would take all of your time in the first response but just part of your time in the second.

In addition, you would use different language for the different ages of the readers.

Task 2

a) Write a list of points to mention concerning safety in the kitchen.
b) Write a list of extra points you would add if writing about safety in the home.

Skill 2: Planning

Here, we offer a planning system in five stages:

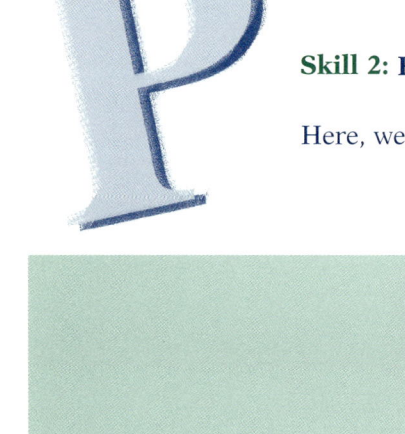

1 **Identify** the purpose and audience – you have learned how to do this.

2 **Brainstorm** the central idea, using a spidergram.

3 **Place** those **ideas into** a **logical order**.

Leave line spaces between each one. Fill these spaces with additional details.

4 **Note down words** and **phrases** you will use in the response: a **palette of vocabulary** you will use to bring your essay to life.

5 **Write your answer** and **check your work**.

Five Stage Planning

Question:
Write a letter to the government, to persuade politicians to give more money to improve IT facilities in schools.

Brainstorm

fewer exclusions
better exam results
teaching tailored more for individuals
appeal to boys?
students enjoy school more
improved staff/student relations

IT FACILITIES

prepare students for the modern world
Internet connections to other schools
use of Internet by more students
encourages private study/self-help
more technological success in the future for Britain

Plan and additional details

Introduction
More money for IT will benefit students, schools and the country

1. Advantages for Students

Students will enjoy school more
IT very popular. Computers in many homes already. Move away from the tedium of writing.

Appeal to boys
Boys love computers. Interest them in learning. Something they do well. Examples from my school. But don't leave out girls.

Better exam results
Response would be immediate. Boys, especially, would achieve more. Packages could be aimed precisely at individual needs.

Would encourage private study/self-help ...

2. Advantages for Schools

Task 3

Complete this plan, using the ideas from the spidergram, and filling in the 'line spaces', as above, with extra details. Add notes for your conclusion.

Vocabulary Palette

Look at this palette of useful words and phrases.

> Nevertheless
>
> However
>
> There are many examples in my own school
>
> Money can be found for wars but perhaps education is less important?
>
> Furthermore
>
> Which countries are improving fastest?
>
> Surely no one could disagree
>
> On the other hand
>
> We have to pledge ourselves to improvement
>
> Contrary to popular opinion

Task 4

Draw your own palette, and write down four potentially useful words and phrases of your own, one from each of the following areas:

- **rhetorical** phrases intended to rouse our emotions ('surely no one could disagree …')

- **ironic** phrases which use **sarcasm** or **humour** ('money can be found for wars but …')

- any phrases you feel will be **effective** ('we must stride forward …')

- **discourse markers** that link ideas (like 'however', 'nevertheless', etc.).

The Invisible Palette
EXAMINER'S TIP!

Of course, in the exam, you may not have time to draw a palette, but jot down key words and phrases, as if from an imaginary palette, ready to 'paint on to' your essay.

Extension Work: The response itself – the IT letter

Skill 3: Writing

Now you should be ready to write the letter. Of course, you will need to set it out properly; but you should find it relatively easy to produce, because most of the hard work has already been done.

However, there are skills to emphasise at this point:

1. **Spelling**
   - Many mistakes can be avoided: look particularly for doubling of letters, use of 'their', 'there', 'they're', etc.
2. **Expression**
   - Don't repeat yourself.
   - Use words and phrases that are appropriate for the intended audience.
3. **Punctuation**
   - Keep re-reading your response as you write it, and correct punctuation.
   - When you pause, consider using a full stop, comma or question mark.
   - If you can use commas, colons and semi-colons properly, show the examiner!
   - Don't forget apostrophes.
4. **Paragraphing**
   - One-sentence paragraphs or very long rambling ones usually suggest this is likely to be an 'E Grade' candidate.
   - Paragraphs that are all the same length usually indicate 'D Grade' work.
   - A variety of paragraph lengths suggest A*–C standard.
   - Paragraphs that contain flowing sentences and are linked well come from the best candidates.

Task 5

Write the first four or five paragraphs of your letter.

Use your plan and keep re-reading the title.

Skill 4: Checking

Task 6

a) Re-read the advice above and correct your response.
b) Count how many improvements you have made!

Examiner's Summary
- You must remember exactly the purpose and audience for which you are writing.
- Take time to produce a detailed plan: it is essential.
- Write carefully. Don't rush.
- Time spent checking your response will improve your mark.
- The more you practise, the easier the Writing Process becomes.

Unit 8 Revising Writing Skills

Target To improve presentational, technical and compositional skills.

Good technical skills = Good grade

Section B of both English papers tests writing skills.
Assessment is made on the content of responses and on your ability to write:
- accurately
- neatly
- fluently.

This unit highlights technical skills needed for better grades.

Spelling: what the levels mean

Grade	Statement	Meaning
'E Grade'	'accurate basic spelling'	Common words spelt correctly
'C Grade'	'spelling generally accurate'	Most spellings correct
'A Grade'	'high level of technical ability'	Very few errors

It is unlikely that you will suddenly improve all spellings overnight, but you can improve in key areas:

1. Ensure you can spell all the words used regularly on your palette.

2. Learn discourse markers, such as 'nevertheless', 'however', etc.

Task 1

Ask a friend to dictate to you the opening paragraph from a text you have studied. Afterwards, mark it together to check for accuracy. If you made a mistake, are you able to identify why you did it (e.g. it sounded like another spelling)?

Borrow Spellings! EXAMINER'S TIP!

For Paper 1, you can **borrow** vocabulary from the texts in Section A – make sure you copy the words correctly.
Try checking your spellings from the last to the first, when you finish writing. This will help you to concentrate on the words, and not the flow of the text.

Punctuation

Grade	Statement	Meaning
'F Grade'	'Generally accurate punctuation of sentences.'	This means using **full stops** and **capital letters**.

To gain higher marks, use a wider range of punctuation, including **commas**.

Task 2

Find a newspaper or magazine, and underline all the commas in three reports. Then read the sentences out loud, noticing how the commas are used. Finally, write three sentences in which you include commas.

Colons
- follow a general statement, to introduce lists
- or introduce quotations.

Semi-colons
- break up complicated lists
- or separate closely related sentences.

Example: I want to be like my father when I'm older: as intelligent as a chess Grand Master; as sophisticated as a member of the aristocracy; and as gentle as a hungry Rottweiler. Of course, he thinks he's nothing special; all fathers are modest. As he says to us at meal-times: "I am but a humble soul ..."

Task 3

Write three sentences, like the ones above, which include colons and semi-colons.

Apostrophes

You will have covered these rules before, but as a quick reminder:

apostrophes of omission – something has been left out, e.g. 'do not' becomes 'don't'; 'I am' becomes 'I'm'.
apostrophes of possession – something is owned, e.g. 'the room of the girl' becomes 'the girl's room'; 'the room of the girls' becomes 'the girls' room'.

Apostrophe Rules REMINDER!

Speech marks

This passage (continued overleaf) will help you to remember the layout and form.

"I can do simple speech marks," said Sadie.
Jamie replied, "I can do them when the name of the person who's speaking comes first."

Layout and Form REMINDER!

Unit 8 *Revising* Writing Skills

"It gets more difficult," said Steph, "when the speaker comes in the middle of the words spoken and is mentioned in the middle of a sentence."
"Sometimes it's slightly easier, though," said Sanjay. "Use a full stop if the speaker is mentioned when one sentence finishes and before the next one starts."
"But don't forget when to close speech marks. Only close them when the speaker finishes, no matter how many sentences she speaks," said Sarah.
"True! And there can only be one speaker in each paragraph," added the teacher.

Task 4

Write ten lines of conversation about the current state of your GCSE work, using the same style of conversation as the one above. Include speech marks and at least four apostrophes.

Question marks	Exclamation marks
You will know when and how to use question marks, but remember that it is easy to forget to use them in the stress of examinations.	Use exclamation marks sparingly, even when writing speech. Some candidates use them too often. You should use them only to indicate: ● suddenness of expression ● surprise ● or to show something is remarkable.

Expression

'C Grade' candidates use words and phrases which are interesting enough to make the reader want to read more.

Vocabulary

You must develop your vocabulary. New words need to be met 'in context' – in stories and articles you read. For English examinations, particularly Paper 1, you can find appropriate words in broadsheet newspapers.

Task 5

a) Find **five** new words each day in the newspaper.
b) Use a dictionary to discover what they mean.
c) Learn them and put them into practice sentences.

Originality

Avoid clichés (phrases we have all heard many times before). Instead, develop new vocabulary, similes or metaphors.

Rather than:
'That soap opera is rubbish. It's like watching paint dry.'
Consider:
'That soap opera is as riveting as assemblies about litter.'

Try to '**show**', rather than '**tell**'.

Rather than:
'I was bored and restless.'
Consider:
'I sat idly flicking through a creased magazine, or wandered up and down the corridor, checking the large cream clock on the dull wall ...'

Task 6

Using the skills above, describe waiting for a train on an empty platform.
- Include two similes and two metaphors of your own.
- Try not to *tell* the reader your feelings, but *show* them in actions or behaviour.

Sentence construction

Notice how a simple sentence can be developed:

1. I love you.
2. Despite your nose, I love you.
3. Despite your nose, which sports more spots than a Dalmatian, I love you.
4. Despite your nose, which sports more spots than a Dalmatian, I love you and everything about you.
5. Despite your nose, which sports more spots than a Dalmatian, I love you and everything about you, especially that big fat wallet packed with money you showed me on Saturday night ...

Task 7

Write a simple sentence about food, then build on to it, like in the example above. Start with: 'I love ...'.

Paragraphing: what the levels mean

Grade	Paragraph Types
'E Grade'	Few paragraphs
'D Grade'	Paragraphs are same length
'C Grade'	Paragraph length varies appropriately for the meaning
'B Grade'	Paragraphs begin to help develop ideas

Notice how stories and articles use paragraphs to make points simply, to describe or to build to a climax. Try to use paragraphs effectively in your own writing.

Final tips

Write two sides, as advised on the examination paper. Writing more can lead to poor presentation.

If you find yourself designing a leaflet or magazine page, do sketching quickly: only handwriting is being assessed.

Presentation
REMEMBER!

Unit 9 Writing to Argue

Targets

1. To learn how to construct an argument.
2. To consider different approaches to argumentative writing.
3. To examine beginnings and endings.
4. To follow the Writing Process.

Skill 1: How to construct an argument

To argue, you must be aware that there is an alternative viewpoint.
Do not just state what you believe; try to counter alternative points that:
- have been made

or
- could be made.

An argument is effective if it convinces the reader or gives the reader cause to reconsider an opinion.

'Writing to Argue' requires:

- a strong beginning and ending
- a logical structure
- details which can be used as 'proof'
- an understanding of the alternative viewpoint
- logic which overcomes that other viewpoint.

FOCUS: Argumentative Writing

Skill 2: Approaches to argumentative writing

There are many possible approaches. Two, in particular, are worth consideration:

- A two-part response which states one case, then counters it with another.
- A piece written from one point of view but which makes reference to an alternative viewpoint, when appropriate.

Skill 3: Beginnings and endings

The most basic organisation for an argumentative piece of writing is:

● Opening: say what your point of view is.	● Middle: argue your case in detail.	● End: sum up by restating your main argument.

However, it is important that:

- the first paragraph is interesting
- the final paragraph is convincing.

Produce interesting and convincing writing

Skill 4: The Writing Process

To be successful, you should follow the routine established in Unit 7 (page 34):

Five Stage Planning

1. Identify the purpose and audience.
2. Brainstorm ideas.
3. Organise ideas.
4. Create a palette of extra details and key phrases.
5. Write your answer and check your work.

Unit 9 Writing to Argue

PRACTICE

Read this question:

Write a speech for a conference about transport, in which you argue that no one should be charged to travel on buses.

Stages 1 and 2

Brainstorm ideas and create a palette (we have helped you in this case).

Brainstorm

FOR CHARGING
- otherwise money needed from tax-payers
- unfair on those who need to use cars
- buses unreliable: would be more so without proper funding
- bus service would collapse
- funding would be taken from health and education?
- something for nothing never works

AGAINST CHARGING
- more would use buses
- safer roads
- more buses so more jobs
- fewer cars so less pollution
- fewer traffic jams
- better bus service would result
- more sociable to travel with others
- better transport policy for new century

Task 1

FOCUS: Using Logic

You decide to answer this question by writing the argument for charging, then putting more strongly the argument against charging.

Write down the points above in a logical order – the order you would choose.

(For this exercise, only concern yourself with organising the above ideas, rather than adding extra notes.)

Now look at this palette of key phrases and words.

Palette

however
nevertheless
in contrast
on the other hand

more consideration for the environment
over-reliance on the motor car
health must come before convenience

Task 2

Copy out this palette and add to it.

Stage 3: Writing

Read this example of a possible opening to the essay:

It is clear that, as a society, we must change our attitude to travel. The car has had its day; environmental considerations are now more important. It is vital that more people begin to use the buses again so that …

FOCUS: Using a Palette

Task 3

Complete the paragraph, then write the first sentence of the next one, covering the first point you placed in your plan.

Now read this ending, which is equally firm:

Politicians are intelligent. In time, they will come to accept that free buses will benefit us all, getting cars off the roads. People will be happy to use them …

Task 4

Add *three* more sentences to this ending, to *sum up* your argument and convince your audience that no one should be charged to travel on a bus.

Interesting & Convincing Writing = Marks
REMEMBER!

PRACTICE **Rhetoric, second-guessing, anecdotes and humour**

If you concentrate on one point of view, and do not include a detailed alternative viewpoint, it allows more:
- time to put your own argument
- space in which to develop your points.

Here are three techniques you can use:

1 Rhetorical questions
These raise the emotions of the reader and do not expect an answer.

Example: *We all know that things need to change, don't we? We have been told about what is happening to the environment; how long will it be before we start to do something about it?*

Task 5

Write one or two sentences in which you use rhetorical questions to support your argument for free buses.

2 Second-guessing
When you predict in advance what the objections might be and answer them.

Example: *Although some might say that giving more public funding to buses will mean less money for the health service, this does not have to be the case …*

As you can see, even though you have mentioned the opposite argument, you can make it seem incorrect.

Task 6

Write a sentence in which you mention the argument for paying bus fares, but make the argument seem incorrect. Start with 'Although' or 'In spite of' or 'Even though'.

3 Anecdotes
Short personal stories or accounts, which, in the case of argumentative writing, could prove your points.

Example: *My grandad could not afford the bus into town and did all his shopping locally. He had to pay more for his food than he would have done at a supermarket. He was poor and even though he had worked hard all his life he had to do without things. Free buses would make such a difference to old people and to poor people in general.*

4 Humour

Finally, a touch of humour, when appropriate, can enliven your writing:

Example: *Of course, my grandad never trusted anybody. He wouldn't have boarded a free bus, in case it didn't have any brakes. He'd have made grandma try it out first ...*

Task 7

Write any paragraph of your response. In it, use both anecdote and humour.

Extension Work: The final response

These are the opening sentences for each paragraph of one response. Notice how the ideas seem to follow logically:

Paragraph 1
Bus travel should be free ...
Paragraph 2
Those in charge of transport policy must realise that free buses would become full buses, because people would abandon cars to save money ...
Paragraph 3
Consequently, jobs would be created: bus drivers would be needed, and ...
Paragraph 4
Such a growth in public transport inevitably leads to improved services ...
Paragraph 5
What is more, travellers would become more sociable; they would no longer be sitting alone in their cars.
Paragraph 6
'Fewer motorists' means 'less pollution'.
Paragraph 7
Not only would the air improve, because there would be fewer traffic jams, but also the roads would be safer for pedestrians.
Paragraph 8
Surely, no one can argue convincingly against obvious improvements?

Task 8

Choose any three consecutive paragraphs and complete them, keeping the opening sentences as they are. Use the skills you have learnt.

Examiner's Summary

- Argue against another viewpoint.
- Use rhetoric, 'second-guessing', anecdote and humour, when appropriate.
- Give special consideration to introductions and conclusions.

Unit 10 Writing to Persuade

Targets
1. To construct a persuasive argument.
2. To use rhetorical and emotive techniques, anecdote and humour.
3. To write an effective opening and ending.

FOCUS: Using Persuasive Language

Some tasks in the exam require you to 'persuade' or use 'persuasion'. This might seem the same as being asked to 'argue' a point. However, there are subtle differences. Generally speaking when you seek to 'persuade' you:

- usually concentrate on one point of view
- tend to be more subjective, more personal, and more one-sided
- try to get a more emotional response from your readers.

However, you do often use similar techniques as those covered in Unit 9, 'Writing to Argue', such as using rhetoric, anecdotes and so on (page 46).

The sorts of questions you might be asked in the exam are as follows.

'Formal' Questions

These are quite close in style and content to an 'argue'-style question, the only difference being, perhaps, that you might not put the other case.

Examples:

'Write a letter to your local council to persuade it to improve health services in your area.'

'Write an article for a national newspaper, to persuade the readers to campaign for closer links with Europe.'

'Write a leaflet to persuade the public to oppose the factory farming of animals.'

Less Formal Questions

These sorts of questions are quite different, and expect a persuasive response to a less contentious (perhaps less serious) subject – one about which few would argue.

Examples:

'Write an article for a teenage magazine. Persuade the readers that your favourite group or singer is the best in the business.'

'Write a speech for your year group, persuading them to help you to raise money for a new youth centre.'

'Write a leaflet to persuade children not to begin smoking.'

Learn persuasive techniques by noticing how those around you persuade others. For example, count the number of different techniques used by a teacher in any lesson; and how parents deal with young children. For example, consider how parents and teachers use warnings.

EXAMINER'S TIP! Copy the 'Persuaders'

Question: You have been corresponding on the Internet with a boy or girl from another country. He or she has asked you to write in person to them. Write a letter to persuade your foreign penfriend to visit you for the summer.

PRACTICE

Brainstorm

- help learn even better English
- chance to see the country
- regret forever if doesn't come
- break from own family

Visit

Task 1

Complete the spidergram.

Unit 10 Writing to Persuade

FOCUS: Planning

Task 2

Organise the ideas into a logical order: the order in which you would write about them.

Remember!

> Ideas should be clustered into sections, so that they have something in common, and follow sensibly from what you have just been saying.

Persuasive Language
Normally, you would now create a palette of extra ideas, words and phrases to use. First, let's look at the language used in persuasive responses.

Read these paragraphs:

1. When here, you will visit many places like Wales, Devon, the Lake District, Stratford-upon-Avon, Edinburgh, York and London. I'll take you to castles like Caernarvon, Leeds and Warwick. You'll have an opportunity to see other countries without paying a penny.

2. Will you ever again have a chance to see so many places that are highlighted in the guidebooks? You can visit Wales, with its own people and traditions; Devon, full of rolling hills and cream teas; the Lake District, once the home of the Romantic Poets; Shakespeare's birthplace in Stratford-upon-Avon; and famous cities such as York, Edinburgh and London. The castles will amaze you: Caernarvon, Leeds, Warwick and many more, equally stunning. You won't have to pay a penny for all this: can you afford to turn down such an offer?

Task 3

Note down any differences between Paragraphs 1 and 2. Think about the use of emotive and rhetorical language, and visual imagery.

Task 4

Now write the palette for your letter – that is, your own selection of key emotive and rhetorical phrases and, where relevant, visual imagery.

There are two other key elements that will help to improve your grade.

PRACTICE

1. The Opening

Naturally, you want to interest the reader, so the use of **anecdote** – a brief story used to prove a point – can be used. It is useful at any stage, but is particularly effective at the start of a persuasive response.

Example

> Dear Lotte,
>
> I am still waiting to hear whether you can come to spend the summer with us. If you can't make up your mind, perhaps the story of what happened to my sister might persuade you.
>
> She was invited to spend two weeks with a family in America when she was sixteen and she had the time of her life. Apart from the fact that she learnt all about what Americans are really like, she also discovered that boys over there love an English accent. She was very popular and had more dates than my grandma eats at Christmas! (I hope you understand English jokes ...)

Task 5

Now write a persuasive anecdote to go at the start of your letter. Add a touch of humour if you can, if it is appropriate.

2. The Ending

Here are two possible types:
1. sum up what you have already said

or

2. produce a final, compelling touch of persuasion.

Type 1: summing up

> I hope I've managed to convince you to come and that you will write soon to say when you'll be arriving. Don't forget: a complete break, sightseeing and new friendships await you. Also, as I said, your English will improve, and you will be more likely to get that job working in a hotel abroad when you are older.
>
> It will be a wonderful holiday. Please come!

Task 6

Write an ending to sum up the points in your letter.

Type 2: compelling ending

> If I haven't yet managed to persuade you to come, you must bear in mind one last point. The biggest music festival Britain has ever seen will be taking place near here in August. Every top act will be appearing: you name them, they'll be there. Don't miss this opportunity! If you come, you'll be the envy of all your friends – and I mean all!

Task 7

Write an ending for your letter that includes a final, powerful point.

Go For A Better Grade!

Extension Work: Improved persuasion

Read this extract – it is 'A Grade' standard. The question asked students to compose a leaflet persuading people to contribute to a charity, called FamAid.

> *Please support our fundraising for FamAid. Across the world, young children are starving and need help from organisations like ours, if they are to survive.*
>
> *On a recent trip to India, I held a tragic young baby who died only minutes later. It is not something a person could ever forget. Can you pretend deaths like this are not happening? Or should we all be involved in creating a more humane world?*
>
> *I believe there is nothing more pitiful than a child's cry but children are crying in half the countries in the world. They cry to us and we must care.*

Task 8

a) Note down the three most effective phrases or sentences.
b) Say whether they are emotive, rhetorical or anecdotal and why they are effective.

Unit 10 Writing to Persuade

Task 9

Read this 'D' standard extract.

> We need a new common room for Year 11 and are raising as much money as we can. You are the Headteacher and I hope you will help us. You could ask parents to give us support. You could ask the school governors as well. I am sure you can see we deserve some help and we are confident you have the influence to get us what we need.

Rewrite the extract, developing the sentences and the extract as a whole, so that it would gain a higher grade.

Get an A Grade by using:
- emotive language
- rhetorical questions
- anecdotes
- and, if possible, humour

Examiner's Summary

Follow the Writing Process you have now learned.

- Use rhetorical questions, emotive language, anecdote, imagery.
- Use humour, where appropriate.
- Make the opening and ending effective.
- Learn the art of persuasion from those around you.

Unit 10 Writing to Persuade

Unit 11 Writing to Advise

Targets
1. To write for a given audience.
2. To structure confident and appropriate advice.
3. To fulfil the Writing Process.

FOCUS: Priorities

Generally, to advise you will have three priorities. You will need to:
- discuss the problem
- persuade the reader that you have the solution
- offer sound advice.

To be convincing, you are often likely to use a style which is slightly less formal than when, for example, you write to argue.

1. Audience

As usual, when given a question, focus on the item, purpose and audience:

Write a <u>letter</u> to a <u>cousin</u> offering <u>advice</u> on what he or she <u>should do next year</u>, <u>after GCSEs</u>.

[audience]

The style you use when advising a cousin is likely to use a different tone and language from that used in a letter to Sky TV to argue that 'The Simpsons' should be shown throughout each afternoon; or to that used to persuade your grandmother to avoid dark alleys when coming home from evening bingo sessions.

At the same time, you must remember that the examiner is rewarding you for your language skills, so you still need to show that you can use complex sentences and a wide range of vocabulary.

EXAMINER'S TIP! Demonstrate Language Skills

> **Response 1**
>
> *Unwise!*
>
> Eddie!
> Oright? How's yer bird? Bin suppin' again? Yer a right one, you.

> **Response 2**
>
> *Better*
>
> Dear Eddie,
> I'm sorry I've not written for ages, but, as you know, my mum's started her new job and life's not been the same since. Our dinner comes cold now with heating instructions. Mum says it'll do us all good …

Task 1

Add another paragraph to Response 2, in the same style. In it, move on to the purpose of your letter.

2. Confident and appropriate advice

If you wish to have your advice accepted, you might decide to:
- list a range of possibilities and decide which one is most sensible
- concentrate on a relatively limited range of options, but tell your audience that a particular decision – or particular decisions – are most advisable.

Whichever method you choose, to seem confident you can use a three-stage method:
- argue your case
- persuade the audience to accept your point of view
- advise them accordingly.

FOCUS: Three-Stage Method

Process

If, therefore, you were writing the letter to your cousin, as your brainstorm you might:
- collect the ideas about what opportunities are available
- structure them so that you first argue against those you favour least
- move to your favoured options last.

That will allow you to develop those ideas, persuade the reader they are most sensible and give more lengthy advice.

> **Task 2**

Produce a spidergram of ideas about what your cousin might do next.

visit careers office   *GNVQ*
A/S Levels

Next move

Sequencing

It is vital that you place your ideas into a logical order, so that each follows sensibly from what has gone before. If you do not 'carry the reader with you', your advice is likely to be ignored.

> **Task 3**

Sequence your ideas for your plan, and add relevant notes under each sub-heading.
An introduction has been done for you:

> 1. **First steps**
> Talk it over with friends and family.
> Visit the careers office/discuss with careers adviser.
> Don't rush the decision.
> Consider what you hope for in 10 years' time.
>
> 2.

Appeal to the reader

Use a Range of Techniques
EXAMINER'S TIP!

As with argument and persuasion, you can appeal to your reader by employing:
- rhetoric
    'After all, what is the point of spending all those years at school and gaining excellent exam passes then deciding to work behind a till in a supermarket for the rest of your days? If you have the chance to take extra courses and become a manager, why not go for it?'

- anecdotes

  'A friend of mine decided GNVQs were the way to go – and she looks set for the brightest future. Last year, she …'

- humour

  'Of course, if you decide to simply drop out, there will always be a place for you round at our house. Though you'll have to share it with Rover.'

Task 4

Note down:
1. **two rhetorical sentences**
2. **two suitable anecdotes**
3. **one example of humour**

which might be useful in your response.

Decide where you will use them in your letter.

The ending

Pay particular attention to what you will include in your final paragraph. It is likely to contain a summary of your advice:

'And so, the decision is yours. You have to decide whether you are going to take the job with the bakery and hope that some sort of NVQ will give you hope for the future; or you can be more positive, talk to the careers service, consider moving to the college and taking the exams we all know you can pass and set out your stall for the rest of your life. I know what your mum and dad want you to do. But don't do it for them. Do it for yourself.'

or make one final, decisive point:

'We both know that you want to work in the music industry. If you are prepared to take the risk, I think I can get you an audition with my uncle's agent – and he will be able to get you work in Europe. You have the talent and I have the contact. I think you should go for it. You have nothing to lose.'

Task 5

Write two sets of notes:
1. A collection of the main ideas that you might include in your conclusion.
2. A final, detailed and decisive point that could be saved and used as an alternative ending.

Discuss the ideas with a friend: decide which would provide the most effective ending.

The palette

As you move on to your palette, you might concentrate on two kinds of discourse markers – those which:
- sequence your ideas
- demonstrate cause and effect.

> *Use discourse markers to support your structure*

For example:

Sequence
Firstly ... in addition ... then ... at the same time ...

Cause and effect
As a result of this ... the effect of this is likely to be that ... this will mean that ...

It is also useful to have a range of phrases to convince the reader.
These might be *relatively subtle*:
Obviously ... It is likely that anyone in this situation would ... It might be worth considering

or you might choose to employ an imperative tone:
Make a decision and stick with it ... Avoid those pitfalls ... Get on with your life!

Task 6

Complete your palette.

Task 7

Write your letter, remembering to be confident and offer clear advice.

Extension work: Top quality advice

This is an extract from an A Grade candidate, writing as an Agony Aunt in a national newspaper and offering advice about relationships:

> 'Above all, consider the future. In the situation in which you find yourselves, it seems easiest to run away, begin your own lives somewhere new and forget all about the parents who are trying to prevent you from enjoying true happiness. However, is it that simple? Will you be able to cope? Just as importantly, will you be able to live with the guilt of what you have put them through?
>
> Think long and hard before grasping for the feather of freedom; it might just float beyond your reach, and you could crash, painfully.'

To be awarded an A Grade, a response must have:
- form, content and style consistently matched to purpose and audience
- a coherent structure, with fluently linked sentences and paragraphs
- a consistent and distinctive style with evidence of conscious crafting
- clear presentation and a high level of accuracy.

The only phrase which is likely to confuse you here is 'conscious crafting'. That is a term used when a candidate demonstrates (in a way that shows thought) his or her ability by using language that is effective, imaginative and, of course, appropriate.

Task 8

Which of these descriptors could be used to describe the extract?

The extract was part of a response to this letter:

> Dear Mave,
>
> My parents say I have to finish with my boyfriend, and his parents hate me. They won't listen to us, and we're thinking of just running away. Should we do it?
>
> Sonya

Task 9

Imagine you are 'Aunt Mave' and have decided to supplement your brief answer in the paper by writing a detailed and more personalised letter to Sonya.

1. plan your response fully: brainstorm, sequence and produce a palette
2. write the letter.

Examiner's Summary

- Use the Writing Process to structure your response.
- Adopt a friendly but informed tone.
- Offer advice which is appropriate and convincing.
- Use a range of techniques.
- Make sure your language suits your purpose.

Unit 12 Writing to Inform

Targets
1. To identify purpose and audience.
2. To plan effectively.
3. To produce an informative response.
4. To develop the response logically and fluently.
5. To fulfil the Writing Process.

Stage 1: Underlining or highlighting
Underlining or highlighting reminds you what is required.
Slight differences in questions make a considerable difference to the response.
What differences would result from the following titles?

1. Write a letter to a *close but ageing* relative to inform them about **how *you intend*** to spend **the summer holidays** following your GCSE exams.

2. Write a letter to a *close* relative to inform them **how, ideally, you *would like*** to spend the **summer holidays** following your GCSE exams.

Stage 2: Structure
Structure is always important. Plan to relay information logically and progressively:

- the opening paragraph should introduce the topic
- following paragraphs should provide development, using discourse markers like: *next, then, subsequently, afterwards, therefore,* etc.
- the response should draw to a definite conclusion.

Stage 3: Relevance
Check that your information is relevant to the title.

For example, if you are informing younger students about the demands of GCSE examinations, do not write about the problems with Key Stage 3 tests.

Impress the examiner with the fluency and organisation of your ideas

Stage 4: Planning
Planning is essential, to ensure that you have not omitted something you later realise is important.

We say: "Oh, I forgot to mention earlier that …", but here you are writing. Details must not be forgotten.

Stage 5: Follow your plan
The writing must follow your plan, to make the flow of your information convincing.

PRACTICE

Read this question:

Write a letter to inform <u>the person who employs you part-time</u> that you <u>have won a travel competition and will be unable to do your job for four weeks.</u>

Task 1

Brainstorm ideas.

apologies *keep job open*
excited
four weeks away

Win!

Task 2

Organise your ideas.
Use the following sub-headings as your plan (they are relevant and could be joined together for a logical and fluent response):

- details about your win and how it will affect your job
- reasons why you wish to accept the voyage you have won
- why you hope the job will be kept open for you
- your feelings about your employer and/or employment
- a conclusion which sums up your feelings about the win and the job.

Plan Using Sub-headings

Task 3

Create your language palette.

Task 4

Next, consider the tone of your letter. Re-read the question, then decide which of these openings is most appropriate, and why:

Example 1
> I have just won a competition and I am going abroad for a month and you will have to keep my job open for me.

Example 2
> I am really excited. I entered a competition with a first prize of a cruise across to Africa: and I have won! Unfortunately, if I go away for four weeks, I will need an extended period of leave from my job. I am hoping that you will realise my trip is an opportunity I can't refuse, and that you might be prepared to keep my job open for me until I return …

61
Unit 12 Writing to Inform

Task 5

Write your own opening.
Make sure it:
- reminds your employer of what, exactly, your job involves
- gives details of the competition
- says when you need to be away
- asks for permission to take an extended holiday.

PRACTICE

You are going to link your opening to the next section of your plan.

Task 6

Write two sentences, either of which could be used to begin your next paragraph, which will give reasons why you wish to accept the voyage you have won.

Begin your sentences with the following discourse markers:
- *Of course,*
- *As you will appreciate,*

Task 7

Choose the best opening sentence, and then write the remainder of the section (this can be one paragraph, or more).

Task 8

Now write the section in which you say why you hope the job will be kept open for you. You will need a sentence which moves you on from what has gone before: for example, '*I understand, however, that all holidays must come to an end*', or something similar. Try to create a link of your own.

Following your linking sentence, you must **inform** your employer exactly
- why you need/want the job
- or how you can help him or her in the long run, if you can keep the job.

Extra Development
EXAMINER'S TIP!

Do not feel that each point in any plan must be covered in a single paragraph. Sometimes further, vital, development will be needed, which will require extra paragraphs.

Task 9

Complete your response, using appropriate linking sentences. Your tone should still be positive but apologetic.

Unit 12 Writing to Inform

Extension Work: Improving the grade

Here, we look at how to improve a 'D Grade' piece of writing.

The following extracts are from students who were asked to write a speech, to inform a group of headteachers what pupils think about the education system. The first is from a 'D Grade' response.

> I have just told you about some school rules that students hate, and now I want to tell you about what we think about school uniform. Some people like it but most people don't like it. It is old fashioned. We don't want to wear ties, because they stifle us. In summer we are much too hot. Also, the colours are terrible. We want to wear things that are cool. We want to wear trainers too.

Task 10

Rewrite the extract, using:
- less repetition (e.g. 'we want')
- better links between sentences
- rhetorical questions and humour.

Below is an 'A Grade' paragraph.

> There are numerous other points about which we might complain. For example, why do we have to start school at nine o'clock? Is it just because our parents want us out of the house so they can go to work? A poll of school students would show clearly that the majority would prefer a system of flexi-time, so that they could work at the time of day which suits them best. Teachers refuse to accept that it is almost impossible to be enthusiastic about French verbs before your breakfast has even reached your stomach; but students know the truth. They know that if the government is serious about raising standards of education, it should allow students to stay in bed until they feel able to cope with school's demands.

Task 11

Identify the ways in which the 'A Grade' candidate followed the advice in Task 10.

Examiner's Summary
- Always plan carefully.
- Ensure your response is informative and that you are answering the question.
- Link ideas effectively.
- Make sure you move smoothly from an introduction to a logical conclusion.
- Fulfil the Writing Process.

Unit 13 Writing to Explain

Targets
1. To identify purpose and audience.
2. To plan the response.
3. To ensure the content is appropriate and engaging.

1 Purpose and Audience
When writing to explain, you will usually concentrate on the **purpose**. You might have to explain how:
- something works or is organised.

But you will probably write about how:
- something or someone has affected you.

So, the **audience** will be the examiner. You can write more personally.

Exemplar Question:
Explain how an <u>incident in your school career</u> has <u>affected your attitude to education</u>.

2 Planning
Brainstorm, then organise your ideas.

EXAMINER'S TIP! Write About What You Know

As a general rule, write about what you know. If it's something you have simply seen on television, you are unlikely to be convincing.

In this case, your response needs:
- an introduction, showing you are dealing with the title
- a series of connected paragraphs, explaining what happened to you
- a conclusion, which explains how you have been affected.

You would also need the usual language palette:
- discourse markers
- and an assortment of other words and phrases.

3 Being appropriate and engaging
Do exactly what you have been asked to do. For example, for the question above, you would **not** write about a friend's experience. Getting the purpose wrong severely affects your mark.

In this case, to make the writing **engaging** (to hold the examiner's attention) you should make the reader:

- feel the incident really happened
- understand exactly what it was like to be there
- believe such an incident must have changed your life.

Emotion and precise details are essential.

Emotion and precise details are essential

PRACTICE

Read this question:
Who is the <u>most interesting person</u> you have ever known? Explain <u>what the person is like or was like</u> and the <u>effect they have had on other people</u>.

The **audience** is the examiner. Notice:
- the **purpose** is to write about someone who is **interesting**
- and you must explain the effect they have on **others**, not just yourself.

This, therefore, is a strange mixture:
- why *you* think they are interesting
- how *others* are affected.

Task 1

Brainstorm and organise the response.

Use these sub-headings to organise your ideas:	● the person ● why they are interesting ● their effect on others
	● the ending: what, exactly, is interesting about the person.

Always try to think of material which is unlikely to be produced by anyone else. It might be an eccentric member of your family; a person from your childhood in another area; or someone who featured in a strange or memorable event.

Be Original
EXAMINER'S TIP!

If you have followed the above bullet points, your response will be **appropriate**.

To make it **engaging**, you might include:
- physical description
- the person's psychological impact on people
- anecdote
- conversation, to help the person 'come to life'
- similes and metaphors
- humour.

Task 2

Write your language palette. Include phrases and details linked to the bullet points above.

PRACTICE

Consider one candidate's opening:

> *I know a very interesting person. I see her every day. She is funny looking and even scares my dog, Snowy. Snowy isn't frightened of anyone else in the world.*

Task 3

a) Write a list of what this candidate is doing right.
b) Rewrite the opening, improving it by using:
- longer, more complex sentences
- precise description of the person.

Now, read another candidate's effort:

> *The first time I saw him, he was talking to a neighbour of ours, who has been in prison. However, the stranger was not frightening at all. He reminded me of one of those weather forecasters you see on the BBC. I guessed he was probably wearing a cardigan under his overcoat.*

Task 4

Write notes in answer to the following questions:
a) How are the sentences constructed and varied?
b) How is the reader supposed to react to the content? For example, did anything make you smile?
c) How is the writer beginning to show this person is interesting?
d) Which is better, the first or second extract? Why?

Task 5

Write your own opening. Bring your character to life.

Consider using ...
- anecdotes
- simile or metaphor
- speech/dialogue
- a paragraph on each person who has been affected

Task 6

Write the main, central, section of your response, i.e. why the person is interesting and how the person affects other people.

Task 7

Write your ending. Include a summary of your feelings and the person's general effect on others. Begin with:
- I always found her amazing, and so did everyone else.

or
- He terrified all of us, every member of the class.

or
- Something similar, to link with what has gone before.

Unit 13 Writing to Explain

Extension Work: A* quality

Read this 'A* Grade' extract:

> What is more, it was not just me who found her behaviour peculiar. Let's face it, any woman who rushes out into the street dressed only in a Union Jack and buys an ice cream for all the children is hardly likely to be considered normal; and when she danced out and started singing hymns to the church congregation as they left one Sunday, you would have had to be there to appreciate how funny it was. The vicar was speechless. Several very well-dressed ladies simply turned round and went back into the church. Most tried to just pretend she didn't exist.
>
> However, you could never ignore Mrs Decanniere. If there was a chance to be with people, she never missed it. She was gregarious as well as completely mad.
>
> I used to feel sorry for her husband as he persuaded her back into the darkness of their little house. He could have left her in an institution, but wanted her at home with him. He must have loved her, despite everything, but she seemed to be wearing him away as the years went by. He went greyer and his eyes became tired, almost desperate in a way. And at night, through the wall, we could sometimes hear him crying with her. Those who mocked her never knew how much sadness there was in that house …

Task 8

Answer the following questions:
a) What do we learn about the writer's attitude to Mrs Decanniere?
b) How many people's reactions to her are included here, and how do they differ?
c) What is the effect of the short paragraph?
d) How does the writer make the woman and where she lives come to life?

Look back at your own response:
- Is it as lively as this one?
- Have you used anecdotes as successfully?
- Have you used a short paragraph for effect?
- Have you explained as clearly as this why the person is interesting?

FOCUS: Sharpening Skills

Task 9

Rewrite a section of your own response, incorporating the skills you have just been examining. Try to make it as good as the extract above.

Examiner's Summary
- Make sure you are doing exactly what the title demands.
- Write about things you have actually experienced.
- Make your writing lively.
- Conclude by summarising your thoughts about the topic.

Unit 14 Writing to Describe

Targets
1. To describe exactly what is specified in the question.
2. To plan carefully.
3. To produce an interesting opening and an appropriate ending.
4. To make the description come to life.
5. To fulfil the Writing Process.

In descriptive writing, three elements are crucial:
- the opening
- the ending
- originality and vividness.

The Opening

Imagine the examiner has been marking scripts for four or five hours each day for three weeks. It is midnight when he or she gets to your paper. You must grab the examiner's attention.

An effective opening paragraph puts you on your way to success.

The Ending

In a description, instead of a formal conclusion, you could end:
- on a dramatic moment
- with a particular revelation
- with someone walking or driving away, into a new or better life
- or ...?

Whatever you choose, your ending should arise from what has gone before. It must be effective because after reading it the examiner awards your mark. It's your final chance to impress.

Originality and Vividness

You can employ:
- your five senses to make a description sharper
- conversation to bring people and situations to life
- similes, metaphors, onomatopoeia and varied vocabulary to add interest
- variety of sentence and paragraph length for effect.

Read this question:
Describe a <u>town or a village or part of a city</u> that <u>you know well</u>.

PRACTICE

Task 1

Decide what you intend to describe.
Notice:
- You are not asked to write about the countryside, the beach, or a school. Or about somewhere you've never visited but that you have seen on television.
- It *must* be a town, village or part of a city you know well.

Task 2

Brainstorm your ideas.
Include details like:

the people
buildings/areas of interest
shops, restaurants and pubs
traffic and road conditions
the effect of the seasons
war memorial

Town

Now organise your sub-headings from the spidergram into a suitable order.

As you put the ideas into a sensible order, jot down, as part of your palette, the discourse markers you are likely to use to link your sections.

Jot Down the Discourse Markers
EXAMINER'S TIP!

Task 3

Produce the rest of your language palette, e.g. good phrases, extra details.

Task 4

The opening: write four short openings to see which works best:

A Conversation:	B Description of the most important feature:	C Atmosphere: at a particular time of year or time of day:	D Description of a person:
a typical conversation between residents or visitors **or** an argument about the place **or** a conversation which mentions matters you will discuss later **or** any other conversation you think is appropriate.	a building **or** a square **or** a road **or** whatever.	describe what is happening and try to capture the place's mood.	choose a person who is at home in the environment and is naturally part of it.

Unit 14 Writing to Describe

PRACTICE

Re-drafting

Task 5

Rewrite *two* of your openings, adding any appropriate features you have left out from the list below:
- use of senses: sight, touch, taste, hearing or smell
- conversation
- simile
- metaphor
- onomatopoeia
- variation of vocabulary (perhaps using local dialect in conversation)
- sentence length for effect.

Redraft Skills Now — EXAMINER'S TIP!

In the exam you won't have time to rewrite; the skills you learn now need to come automatically on the day.

Task 6

Select the better opening.

Task 7

Write the central sections of your response.
Keep the above list in mind and do not forget you are trying to impress a tired examiner! As you transform your plan into essay form, vary your paragraph length. Try using:

- **short paragraphs**
to make actions seem more dramatic, or to highlight a specific idea or change of pace.

- **longer paragraphs**
to convey a slower, more reflective mood, or when you are describing things in more detail. Also they are useful as a build-up of connected ideas or short phrases, for example in a chase.

The ending

Task 8

Write your ending.
Your final paragraph should grow naturally from what has gone before.
You might, for example, end with:
- a quotation about the place and, perhaps, some comment on it
- your personal feelings about the place
- an image that captures what you have put across in your response
- or a statement about why people stay/leave or why visitors return/don't return.

Extension Work: Improving further

The following response received a top grade.

> The town is vibrant. It hums with a music all its own. Babies cry, like they do anywhere; and men with red faces fall out of the bars into grey Saturday afternoons and laugh too loudly like clowns at the circus; and cars full of young people drive too fast; and things rattle and crash. But all the time there is an undercurrent. This is a town that knows what it is and where it's going. It is moving forward, it is expanding, and the young and the old know they are taking on the world and they are winning.
>
> 'This is the best town in the world,' said a teenager I met outside the new Riddings Centre.
>
> As she moved on, into the concrete and glass structure that towered above us, blue and white in the sunshine, it was hard to disagree.

Task 9

Write down the most effective examples of:

- sentence construction
- use of paragraphs
- metaphor
- simile
- speech
- onomatopoeia

Say what makes each example effective.

Task 10

Write a few short paragraphs about an exciting place you know. Imitate the style of the passage above.

Examiner's Summary

- Answer the question that has been set.
- Fulfil the Writing Process.
- Ensure you have a strong beginning and ending.
- Make the response interesting.
- Concentrate on vocabulary, sentence length and paragraphing.

Unit 15 Revising Poetry from Different Cultures and Traditions

Targets

1. To learn how to:
   - revise the poems
   - quote and make points appropriately
   - link the poems.
2. To practise answering exam questions.

Revising the poems

You will have read many or all of the Poems from Different Cultures in the Anthology. Some you will have studied in more depth.

In the examination, on Paper 2 Section B, you will be required to write about two or three of the poems in 45 minutes. In other words, you will have to be able to deal with each poem in about 15 or 20 minutes. It is vital, therefore, that you
- are well prepared
- have decided which poems you hope to write about
- know what you are likely to be asked about in the exam.

The questions are always likely to focus on three areas:
1. the poems' content
2. the poems' structures
3. the techniques used by the poets.

Focus on the three vital considerations

Revise by Analysing
EXAMINER'S TIP!

Content: topic, the details included to illustrate the situation or ideas and the poet's message.

Structure: how the poem is set out on the page, verse form, line and stanza lengths and the general organisation of the poem.

Techniques: imagery, similes and metaphors, alliteration, onomatopoeia, enjambement, personification, rhythm and rhyme, effective vocabulary, punctuation, contrasts, exaggeration, approaches to purpose and audience.

Task 1

Choose your favourite poem and make notes on its content, structure and linguistic techniques.

Task 2

Although it will take time, repeat the exercise for all the poems you are hoping to write about – that will apply your mind to the areas with which you will have to deal in the exam itself.

In the exam, you must choose one of two questions – one poem from the Anthology will be named in each question. You will have to write about it and another (or others) of your choice. If it is not one of the poems you have prepared well, you can concentrate more of your time on the other poem(s). However, you must prepare as many poems as possible.

Task 3

Read the other poems thoroughly. Concentrate on:
- what they say
- how they say it.

FOCUS: Concentrated Revision

Quoting and making points appropriately

Although you have to work so swiftly in the exam, the basic technique for dealing with literature still applies:
1. make a point
2. quote to prove what you are saying
3. explain the point.

Technique is Vital — EXAMINER'S TIP!

> '*Limbo* gives an impression of life for the slaves: ——▶ *point*
>   'stick is the whip
>   and the dark deck is slavery' ——▶ *quotation*
>
> Brathwaite uses the sound of the beating ('stick/whip'), the dismal alliteration of 'd's and the vision of darkness to capture the horror of the situation ...' ——▶ *explanation*

If you are quoting just three or four words, use quotation marks but absorb the words within your sentence:

> 'When Brathwaite concludes with "on the burning ground", we have to decide whether the narrator reaches a sunny heaven or the fires of hell ...'

For longer quotations:
- be as brief as possible
- indent
- retain the lines of poetry:

> 'At first, the ending of the poem seems optimistic:
> "sun coming up
> and the drummers are praising me".'

Task 4

Choose any poem and explain its message.

Remember to:
- make a point, quote and explain
- set out quotations properly.

Linking poems

Because you will have to link poems in your answer, revise them in pairs or clusters.

Look at content, structure and technique

Decide how your chosen poems can be linked.

You might consider:
- change
- people
- identity
- the politics of cultures
- traditions
- how cultures differ

and:
- narrative voices
- non-standard English
- imagery
- descriptive touches
- the presentation of the verse.

Task 5

Cluster the poems you know in a variety of possible groups.

When comparing poems, consider a simple format for your response:
1. brief introduction: poems chosen and general link
2. an analysis of Poem 1
3. an analysis of Poem 2, referring back to Poem 1 to make comparisons…
4. brief conclusion: similarities/differences.

You are likely to require a stock of comparative words and phrases:

Similarly …   On the other hand …   Whereas …   Although …
The difference in Poem 1 is …   In contrast …   Just as … so …

and so on.

The more you practise writing detailed responses, comparing poems in just 45 minutes, the better will be your examination performance.

Task 6

Choose three poems that deal with situations in which people are not happy. Compare the:
- content
- structures
- techniques used by the poets.

Extension work

Practise your examination techniques on the following titles:

1. How are different cultures reflected in 'Presents from my Aunts in Pakistan' and any other poem?

2. Compare the narrator's attitude in 'Nothing's Changed' with that of an individual from another poem in the selection.

3. Explain how 'Hurricane Hits England' presents us with someone coming to terms with life in a different country and how people react to their surroundings in two other poems.

Examiner's Summary

- Prepare by putting poems in logical groups.
- Know the poems well.
- Be prepared to write about content, structure and techniques.
- Quote effectively.
- Make comparisons clear.
- Practise producing answers in 45 minutes.

Unit 16 Final Revision for English

Targets
1. To be well prepared to answer both examination papers.
2. To focus on what is being tested.
3. To understand the skills required for success.

This Unit deals with the period leading up to the exam, and 'last-minute' revision.

Dealing with Paper 1, Section A

1 Revise the technical vocabulary you need to answer the questions.
Make sure you know:
- the meaning of each technical term (e.g. columns, subjective, rhetorical, etc.)
- the correct spellings
- how to use these words in sentences ('rhetoric' is the noun, 'rhetorical' the adjective).

2 Read non-fiction and media texts regularly.
In each one decide:
- how facts and opinions are used
- how the argument is constructed.

Make notes on:
- audience and message
- layout/presentation
- language
- purpose.

3 Set yourself questions and answer from your notes.
Imagine there are 6 marks for the question and write your answer in 12 minutes. Make sure you quote from the text to prove your points.

4 Think about using the hour for Section A effectively.
Remember you must:
- read the texts carefully
- answer what is asked
- be guided by bullet points when they are used
- check how many marks are given for each question and divide up your time accordingly.

Dealing with Paper 2, Section A

1. Re-read regularly the poems you have studied.
When you begin the examination paper you should:
- be able to choose immediately which poems to write about, because you know them so well
- not have to read the poems – just use them to find suitable quotations.

2. Poetic techniques.
- Check you understand the poetic techniques you have been taught or have noted on your poems and how they make a poem more effective: e.g. an alliteration of 'd' sounds might give the impression of drumbeats.
- Do not just spot the techniques – always explain their use in each case.

Know Your Techniques
EXAMINER'S TIP!

Practice and preparation

1. **Remember** You will: • have two questions on the poems, but should **answer only one** • be asked about **at least two poems in each question** • have to answer on one 'named poem', and another of your choice.	2. **Decide** which poems: • seem to 'go together': plan to write about them as a pair • you would most like to write about – if they 'come up' on the paper, you will be prepared for success.
3. **Write 45-minute practice answers** focusing on meanings and techniques. Write: • a brief introduction • about each poem • a brief conclusion.	4. **Think about what might be asked** Be prepared for: • unexpected questions, by knowing the poems well • bullet points: if they are offered, use them to guide your ideas • questions that expect more than simple meanings: you will be asked about the poems' messages, rather than the story; how the poet puts across a message; or differences between poems.

The Actual Exam

Remember, the question is likely to mention different cultures and/or traditions. Make sure you are prepared for that 'angle'.

Make sure you:
- answer the question set
- concentrate on one poem at a time:
  make comparisons as you write about the second one
- quote briefly
- analyse, do not just say what happens.

Dealing with Paper 1 and Paper 2, Section B

1. Revise approaches to the questions
Make sure you know how to:
- use the Writing Process
- write to argue, persuade, advise, inform, explain and describe
- use layouts appropriately, e.g. articles, leaflets, letters, etc.

If necessary, redo Units from this book.

2. Read any available material
- See how the writing is structured.
- Notice how writers use technical effects, like sentence structure, similes and metaphors.
- Note down useful discourse markers ('moreover', 'as I have said', etc.).

3. Write short extracts to practise for each question
For example, produce extracts from:
- an article for a local paper, **arguing** that teenagers should receive more pocket money
- a letter, to **persuade** your friend to lend you money
- a speech offering **advice** to school students on how to cope with problem teachers
- a leaflet, **informing** teenagers about the dangers of drugs
- a statement to the police, in which you **explain** why your friend was leaving a shop with Cliff Richard's latest CD under his coat
- your autobiography, where you **describe** the happiest moment of your life.

4 Think about how to cope in the examination
Remember you will:
- select one question to answer
- plan, write and check
- pause every half page and ensure you are still answering the question
- use the time appropriately.

Final Reminders

Paper 1, Section A
1. Answer all the questions set.
2. Underline on your question paper, if it helps.
3. Spend 2 minutes per mark.
4. Answer all the bullet points.
5. Prove what you say.

FOCUS
Argue
Persuade
Advise
Inform
Explain
Describe

Paper 2, Section A
1. Answer only:
   - one question
   - the question set.
2. Divide your time between the poems.
3. Write about techniques, not just what happens.
4. Quote, but briefly.

Section B Questions
1. Choose one question.
2. Answer the question set.
3. Always use the Writing Process.
4. Spend:
   - 5 minutes planning
   - 35 minutes writing
   - 5 minutes checking.
5. Write two sides.

Finally
Enter the examination room properly prepared and you will feel in control. The skills in this book can help you to success: you have practised them – demonstrate them on the big day.
Examiners want to award good marks – give them the opportunity!

Good Luck!

Unit 16 Final Revision for English

Your Final Checklist

Check through this list to see that you have covered all the necessary skills and revision areas. The right-hand column tells you which Unit you can go back to, where relevant, if you need to redo or relearn a skill.

	YES	NO	GO TO UNIT
Do you know?			
● The date and time of each examination			–
● What each examination involves (e.g. how many papers, how long, etc.)			1 & 16
● For which examination you need to bring your Anthology			1 & 16
Have you?			
● Learned how to divide up your time in the examination			16
● Read a range of non-fiction and media material			2 & 3
● Noticed how it is presented			3 & 4
● Learned to recognise fact and opinion and how they are used			2
● Learned the technical vocabulary you will need in Paper 1, Section A			5
● Practised comparing texts, using bullet points to guide you			4
● Revised your presentational, technical and compositional skills			8
● Learned the technical terms relating to poetry			15
● Decided which poems you would like to write about			15
● Practised by answering likely questions on the poetry			15
Can you ...?			
● Write appropriately for different purposes and audiences			7
● Plan an essay quickly and effectively			7
● Put together a palette of appropriate words, phrases and discourse markers			7
● Argue effectively			9
● Persuade effectively			10
● Advise effectively			11
● Inform clearly			12
● Explain precisely and effectively			13
● Describe, bringing your description to life			14
● Check and appropriately correct your writing			7 & 8
Finally ...			
● Do you know what makes the difference between one grade and another?			2–14